CREEPY CREATURES

AXOLOTLS

BY ABBY DOTY

WWW.APEXEDITIONS.COM

Copyright © 2025 by Apex Editions, Mendota Heights, MN 55120. All rights reserved. No part of this book may be reproduced or utilized in any form or by any means without written permission from the publisher.

Apex is distributed by North Star Editions:
sales@northstareditions.com | 888-417-0195

Produced for Apex by Red Line Editorial.

Photographs ©: Shutterstock Images, cover, 1, 4–5, 9, 10–11, 12 (top), 12 (bottom), 13, 14–15, 18–19, 21, 28–29; iStockphoto, 6–7, 16–17, 20, 26–27; Blickwinkel/Hartl/Alamy, 22–23, 24

Library of Congress Control Number: 2024940531

ISBN
979-8-89250-319-8 (hardcover)
979-8-89250-357-0 (paperback)
979-8-89250-431-7 (ebook pdf)
979-8-89250-395-2 (hosted ebook)

Printed in the United States of America
Mankato, MN
012025

NOTE TO PARENTS AND EDUCATORS
Apex books are designed to build literacy skills in striving readers. Exciting, high-interest content attracts and holds readers' attention. The text is carefully leveled to allow students to achieve success quickly. Additional features, such as bolded glossary words for difficult terms, help build comprehension.

CHAPTER 1
CLOSE CALL 4

CHAPTER 2
STRANGE SALAMANDERS 10

CHAPTER 3
LIFE IN THE WILD 16

CHAPTER 4
LIFE CYCLE 22

COMPREHENSION QUESTIONS • 28
GLOSSARY • 30
TO LEARN MORE • 31
ABOUT THE AUTHOR • 31
INDEX • 32

CHAPTER 1

CLOSE CALL

A small axolotl swims through muddy water. It is trying to escape a larger fish. But the fish is quick. It chomps down on the axolotl's leg.

Axolotls can swim up to 10 miles per hour (16 km/h).

The axolotl squirms away. But it loses its leg. The hurt animal swims to the bottom of the lake. It changes its skin color to match the sand.

An axolotl's skin has spots. They help the axolotl blend in with rocks and sand.

FAST FACT
Wild axolotls can make their skin a bit lighter or darker.

Finally, the fish swims away. The axolotl is safe. Now, its leg can grow back. After about 50 days, the new limb is ready.

NEW PARTS

Axolotls can regenerate body parts. They can grow new limbs, bones, and **organs**. They can even regrow parts of their brains. The process can take a few weeks or months.

An axolotl can regrow the same body part several times.

CHAPTER 2

STRANGE SALAMANDERS

Axolotls are a kind of salamander. They live underwater. Most are about 10 inches (25 cm) long. They can weigh up to 8 ounces (227 g).

10

Wild axolotls have dark, brownish-gray skin. The color helps them hide in muddy water.

Young salamanders (top) may look very different from adults (bottom).

Most kinds of salamanders go through **metamorphosis**. At first, they have **gills** and fins. They live in the water. Then, their bodies change.

FAST FACT
Long fins and webbed toes help young salamanders move through water.

An axolotl has three pairs of gills. The gills stick out on both sides of its head.

Most adult salamanders lose their gills and fins. They live partly on land. Axolotls are different. Adults keep their gills. They also keep their webbed toes and long fins.

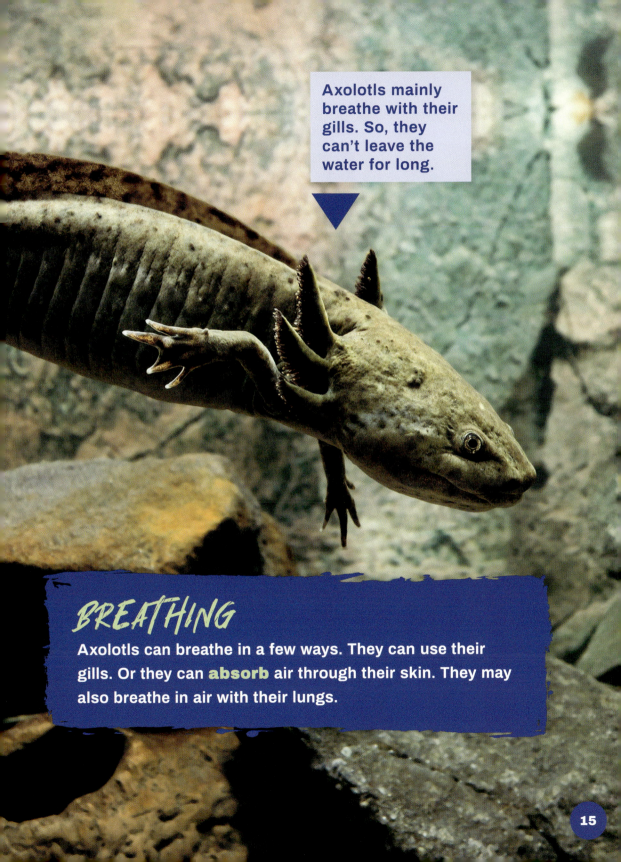

Axolotls mainly breathe with their gills. So, they can't leave the water for long.

BREATHING

Axolotls can breathe in a few ways. They can use their gills. Or they can **absorb** air through their skin. They may also breathe in air with their lungs.

CHAPTER 3

LIFE IN THE WILD

Axolotls are active at night. The animals crawl along lake beds and suck up food. They may eat worms, insects, or small fish.

16

An axolotl sometimes sucks up gravel. The rocks help grind up food in the axolotl's stomach.

For thousands of years, wild axolotls lived in lakes near Mexico City, Mexico. But most of those lakes are gone. Now, axolotls live in the **swamps** and waterways that remain.

FAST FACT
Axolotls are important to Mexican **culture**. People used the creatures for food and medicine.

Some wild axolotls live in Lake Xochimilco in Mexico. But people have built over parts of the lake.

19

Axolotls lived in Lake Chalco before it was drained.

Axolotl **habitats** are in danger. People have drained lakes and made them dirty. Wild axolotls nearly died out. But people are working to save them. They clean the water and make safe places for axolotls to live.

NEW FISH

Axolotls used to have few **predators**. That changed in the 1970s. People brought carp and tilapia to Mexico City's water. These fish eat axolotls.

By the 2020s, most living axolotls were pets. There were fewer than 1,000 left in the wild.

CHAPTER 4

LIFE CYCLE

Axolotls spend most of their lives alone. But they come together to **mate**. Each female lays hundreds of eggs at a time.

An axolotl may lay eggs several times in one year.

FAST FACT
Some animals eat axolotl eggs. So, female axolotls hide the eggs to make them harder to find.

The eggs hatch two weeks later. Babies have tails but no legs. Within hours, they begin to hunt and eat.

Axolotls may hide their eggs among underwater plants or rocks.

Two weeks after hatching, axolotls grow front legs. Back legs develop a couple weeks later. The animals can begin having their own babies after about a year.

SURVIVORS

Axolotls can live for up to 15 years. Growing new body parts helps them survive. Many scientists study axolotls. They hope to learn things that can help humans heal from wounds.

Axolotls reach their full size after about two years.

COMPREHENSION QUESTIONS

Write your answers on a separate piece of paper.

1. Write a few sentences explaining the main ideas of Chapter 3.

2. Which fact about axolotls do you find most interesting? Why?

3. Which animals might an axolotl eat?
    - A. worms
    - B. carp
    - C. salamanders

4. What might happen if axolotls lost their gills and fins like other salamanders?
    - A. They might move faster in water.
    - B. They might live on land.
    - C. They might eat more food.

5. What does **regenerate** mean in this book?

*Axolotls can **regenerate** body parts. They can grow new limbs, bones, and organs. They can even regrow parts of their brains.*

- **A.** break something down
- **B.** replace something lost
- **C.** find more of something

6. What does **develop** mean in this book?

*Two weeks after hatching, axolotls grow front legs. Back legs **develop** a couple weeks later.*

- **A.** to shrink
- **B.** to swim
- **C.** to form

Answer key on page 32.

GLOSSARY

absorb
To take in.

culture
A group's way of living, including the art made by its people.

gills
Body parts that animals use to breathe underwater.

habitats
The places where animals normally live.

mate
To form a pair and come together to have babies.

metamorphosis
A change from a young form to a different adult form.

organs
Parts of the body that do certain jobs. Organs include the heart, lungs, and kidneys.

predators
Animals that hunt and eat other animals.

swamps
Areas of low land covered in water, often with many plants.

BOOKS

Grack, Rachel. *Axolotls*. Minneapolis: Bellwether Media, 2023.

Grodzicki, Jenna. *Axolotl*. Minneapolis: Bearport Publishing, 2024.

Jaycox, Jaclyn. *Axolotls*. North Mankato, MN: Capstone Publishing, 2023.

ONLINE RESOURCES

Visit **www.apexeditions.com** to find links and resources related to this title.

ABOUT THE AUTHOR

Abby Doty is a writer, editor, and booklover from Minnesota.

INDEX

C
culture, 18

E
eggs, 22, 25

F
fins, 12–14

G
gills, 12, 14–15

H
habitats, 20

L
lungs, 15

M
mating, 22
metamorphosis, 12
Mexico City, Mexico, 18, 21

O
organs, 8

P
predators, 21

S
salamanders, 10, 12–14
skin, 6–7, 15
swamps, 18

T
tilapia, 21

ANSWER KEY:
1. Answers will vary; 2. Answers will vary; 3. A; 4. B; 5. B; 6. C